Gallery Books
Editor: Peter Fallon

CREDITING POETRY

Seamus Heaney

CREDITING POETRY

Gallery Books

Crediting Poetry
is first published
on 12 December 1995.

The Gallery Press
Loughcrew
Oldcastle
County Meath
Ireland

ISBN 1 85235 184 5

The author and publisher acknowledge the assistance of the Museum of Sparta, the Embassy of Greece, Dublin, and the Embassy of Ireland, Athens.

The Gallery Press receives financial assistance from An Chomhairle Ealaíon / The Arts Council, Ireland, and The Arts Council of Northern Ireland.

CREDITING
POETRY

When I first encountered the name of the city of Stockholm, I little thought that I would ever visit it, never mind end up being welcomed to it as a guest of the Swedish Academy and the Nobel Foundation. At that particular time, such an outcome was not just beyond expectation: it was simply beyond conception. In the nineteen-forties, when I was the eldest child of an ever-growing family in rural County Derry, we crowded together in the three rooms of a traditional thatched farmstead and lived a kind of den-life which was more or less emotionally and intellectually proofed against the outside world. It was an intimate, physical, creaturely existence in which the night sounds of the horse in the stable beyond one bedroom wall mingled with the sounds of adult conversation from the kitchen beyond the other. We took in everything that was going on, of course — rain in the trees, mice on the ceiling, a steam train rumbling along the railway line one field back from the house — but we took it in as if we were in the doze of hibernation. Ahistorical, pre-sexual, in suspension between the archaic and the modern, we were as susceptible and impressionable as the drinking water that stood in a bucket in our scullery: every time a passing train made the earth shake, the surface of that water used to ripple delicately, concentrically, and in utter silence.

But it was not only the earth that shook for us: the air around and above us was alive and signalling too. When a wind stirred in the beeches, it also stirred an aerial wire attached to the topmost branch of the chestnut tree. Down it swept, in through a hole bored in the corner of the kitchen window, right on into the innards of our wireless set where a little pandemonium of burbles and squeaks would suddenly give way to the voice of a BBC newsreader speaking out of the unexpected like a *deus ex machina*. And that voice too we could hear in our bedroom, transmitting from beyond and behind the voices of the adults in the kitchen; just as we could often hear, behind and beyond every voice, the frantic, piercing signalling of morse code.

We could pick up the names of neighbours being spoken in the local accents of our parents, and in the resonant English tones of the newsreader the names of bombers and of cities bombed, of war fronts and army divisions, the numbers of planes lost and of prisoners taken, of casualties suffered and advances made; and always, of course, we would pick up too those other, solemn and oddly bracing words, 'the enemy' and 'the allies'. But even so, none of the news of these world-spasms entered me as terror. If there was something ominous in the newscaster's tones, there was something torpid about our understanding of what was at stake; and if there was something culpable about such political ignorance in that time and place, there was something positive about the security I inhabited as a result of it.

The wartime, in other words, was pre-reflective time for me. Pre-literate too. Pre-historical in its way. Then as the years went on and my listening became more deliberate, I would climb up on an arm of our big sofa to get my ear closer to the wireless speaker. But it was still not the news that interested me; what I was after was the thrill of story, such as a detective serial about a British special agent called Dick Barton or perhaps a radio adaptation of one of Capt. W. E. Johns's adventure tales about an RAF flying ace called Biggles. Now that the other children were older and there was so much going on in the kitchen, I had to get close to the actual radio set in order to concentrate my hearing, and in that intent proximity to the dial I grew familiar with the names of foreign stations, with Leipzig and Oslo and Stuttgart and Warsaw and, of course, with Stockholm.

I also got used to hearing short bursts of foreign languages as the dial hand swept round from BBC to Radio Éireann, from the intonations of London to those of Dublin, and even though I did not understand what was being said in those first encounters with the gutturals and sibilants of European speech, I had already begun a journey into the wideness of the world. This in turn became a journey into the wideness of language, a journey where each point of arrival — whether in one's poetry or one's life — turned out to be a stepping stone rather than a destination, and it is that journey which has brought me now to this honoured spot. And yet the platform here feels more like a space station than a stepping stone, so that is why, for once in my life, I am permitting myself the luxury of walking on air.

❧

I credit poetry for making this space-walk possible. I credit it immediately because of a line I wrote fairly recently encouraging myself (and whoever else might be listening) to 'walk on air against your better judgement'. But I credit it ultimately because poetry can make an order as true to the impact of external reality and as sensitive to the inner laws of the poet's being as the ripples that rippled in and rippled out across the water in that scullery bucket fifty years ago. An order where we can at last grow up to that which we stored up as we grew. An order which satisfies all that is appetitive in the intelligence and prehensile in the affections. I credit poetry, in other words, both for being itself and for being a help, for making possible a fluid and restorative relationship between the mind's centre and its circumference, between the child gazing at the word 'Stockholm' on the face of the radio dial and the man facing the faces that he meets in Stockholm at this most privileged moment. I credit it because credit is due to it, in our time and in all time, for its truth to life, in every sense of that phrase.

∾

To begin with, I wanted that truth to life to possess a concrete reliability, and rejoiced most when the poem seemed most direct, an upfront representation of the world it stood in for or stood up for or stood its ground against. Even as a schoolboy, I loved John Keats's ode 'To Autumn' for being an ark of the covenant between language and sensation; as an adolescent, I loved Gerard Manley Hopkins for the intensity of his exclamations which were also equations for a rapture and an ache I didn't fully know I knew until I read him; I loved Robert Frost for his farmer's accuracy and his wily down-to-earthness; and Chaucer too for much the same reasons. Later on I would find a different kind of accuracy, a moral down-to-earthness to which I responded deeply and always will, in the war poetry of Wilfred Owen, a poetry where a New Testament sensibility suffers and absorbs the shock of the new century's barbarism. Then later again, in the pure consequence of Elizabeth Bishop's style, in the sheer obduracy of Robert Lowell's and in the barefaced confrontation of Patrick Kavanagh's, I encountered further reasons for believing in poetry's ability — and responsibility — to say what happens, to 'pity the planet', to be 'not concerned with Poetry'.

This temperamental disposition towards an art that was earnest and devoted to things as they are was corroborated by the experience of having been born and brought up in Northern Ireland and of having lived with that place even though I have lived out of it for the past quarter of a century. No place in the world prides itself more on its vigilance and realism, no place considers itself more qualified to censure any flourish of rhetoric or extravagance of aspiration. So, partly as a result of having internalized these attitudes through growing up with them, and partly as a result of growing a skin to protect myself against them, I went for years half-avoiding and half-resisting the opulence and extensiveness of poets as different as Wallace Stevens and Rainer Maria Rilke; crediting insufficiently the crystalline inwardness of Emily Dickinson, all those forked lightnings and fissures of association; and missing the visionary strangeness of Eliot. And these more or less costive attitudes were fortified by a refusal to grant the poet any more licence than any other citizen; and they were further induced by having to conduct oneself as a poet in a situation of ongoing political violence and public expectation. A public expectation, it has to be said, not of poetry as such but of political positions variously approvable by mutually disapproving groups.

In such circumstances, the mind still longs to repose in what Samuel Johnson once called with superb confidence 'the stability of truth', even as it recognizes the destabilizing nature of its own operations and enquiries. Without needing to be theoretically instructed, consciousness quickly realizes that it is the site of variously contending discourses. The child in the bedroom listening simultaneously to the domestic idiom of his Irish home and the official idioms of the British broadcaster while picking up from behind both the signals of some other distress, that child was already being schooled for the complexities of his adult predicament, a future where he would have to adjudicate among promptings variously ethical, aesthetical, moral, political, metrical, sceptical, cultural, topical, typical, post-colonial and, taken all together, simply impossible. So it was that I found myself in the mid-nineteen-seventies in another small house, this time in County Wicklow south of Dublin, with a young family of my own and a slightly less imposing radio set, listening to the rain in the trees and to the news of bombings closer to home — not only those by the Provisional IRA in Belfast but equally atrocious assaults in Dublin by loyalist paramilitaries from the north. Feeling puny in my predicaments as I read about the tragic logic of Osip Mandelstam's fate in the 1930s, feeling challenged yet steadfast in my non-combatant status when I heard, for example, that one particularly sweet-natured school friend had been interned without trial because he was suspected of having been involved in a political killing. What I was longing for was not quite stability but an active escape from the quicksand of relativism, a way of crediting poetry without anxiety or apology. In a poem called 'Exposure' I wrote then:

> If I could come on meteorite!
> Instead, I walk through damp leaves,
> Husks, the spent flukes of autumn,
>
> Imagining a hero
> On some muddy compound,
> His gift like a slingstone
> Whirled for the desperate.
>
> How did I end up like this?
> I often think of my friends'
> Beautiful prismatic counselling
> And the anvil brains of some who hate me

As I sit weighing and weighing
My responsible *tristia*.
For what? For the ear? For the people?
For what is said behind-backs?

Rain comes down through the alders,
Its low conducive voices
Mutter about let-downs and erosions
And yet each drop recalls

The diamond absolutes.
I am neither internee nor informer;
An inner émigré, grown long-haired
And thoughtful; a wood-kerne

Escaped from the massacre,
Taking protective colouring
From bole and bark, feeling
Every wind that blows;

Who, blowing up these sparks
For their meagre heat, have missed
The once in a lifetime portent,
The comet's pulsing rose.

from *North*

In one of the poems best known to students in my genera-
tion, a poem which could be said to have taken the nutrients
of the symbolist movement and made them available in
capsule form, the American poet Archibald MacLeish
affirmed that 'Poetry should be equal to / not true'. As a
defiant statement of poetry's gift for telling truth but telling
it slant, this is both cogent and corrective. Yet there are

times when a deeper need enters, when we want the poem to be not only pleasurably right but compellingly wise, not only a surprising variation played upon the world, but a re-tuning of the world itself. We want the surprise to be transitive, like the impatient thump which unexpectedly restores the picture to the television set, or the electric shock which sets the fibrillating heart back to its proper rhythm. We want what the woman wanted in the prison queue in Leningrad, standing there blue with cold and whispering for fear, enduring the terror of Stalin's régime and asking the poet Anna Akhmatova if she could describe it all, if her art could be equal to it. And this is the want I too was experiencing in those far more protected circumstances in County Wicklow when I wrote the lines I have just quoted, a need for poetry that would merit the definition of it I gave a few moments ago, as an order 'true to the impact of external reality and . . . sensitive to the inner laws of the poet's being'.

◠

The external reality and inner dynamic of happenings in Northern Ireland between 1968 and 1974 were symptomatic of change, violent change admittedly, but change nevertheless, and for the minority living there, change had been long overdue. It should have come early, as the result of the ferment of protest on the streets in the late sixties, but that was not to be and the eggs of danger which were always incubating got hatched out very quickly. While the Christian moralist in oneself was impelled to deplore the atrocious nature of the IRA's campaign of bombings and killings, and the 'mere Irish' in oneself was appalled by the ruthlessness of the British Army on occasions like Bloody Sunday in Derry in 1972, the minority citizen in oneself, the one who had grown up conscious that his group was distrusted and discriminated against in all kinds of official and unofficial ways, this citizen's perception was at one with the poetic truth of the situation in recognizing that if life in Northern Ireland were ever really to flourish, change had to take place. But that citizen's perception was also at one with the truth in recognizing that the very brutality of the means by which the IRA was pursuing change was destructive of the trust upon which new possibilities would have to be based.

Nevertheless, until the British government caved in to the strong-arm tactics of the Ulster loyalist workers after the Sunningdale Conference in 1974, a well-disposed mind could still hope to make sense of the circumstances, to balance what was promising with what was destructive and do what W. B. Yeats had tried to do half a century before, namely, 'to hold in a single thought reality and justice'. After 1974, however, for the twenty long years between then and the ceasefires of August 1994, such a hope proved impossible. The violence from below was then productive of nothing but a retaliatory violence from above, the dream of justice became subsumed into the callousness of reality, and people settled in to a quarter century of life-waste and spirit-waste, of hardening attitudes and narrowing possibilities that were the natural result of political solidarity, traumatic suffering and sheer emotional self-protectiveness.

∾

One of the most harrowing moments in the whole history of the harrowing of the heart in Northern Ireland came when a minibus full of workers being driven home one January evening in 1976 was held up by armed and masked men and the occupants of the van ordered at gunpoint to line up at the side of the road. Then one of the masked executioners said to them, 'Any Catholics among you, step out here.' As it happened, this particular group, with one exception, were all Protestants, so the presumption must have been that the masked men were Protestant paramilitaries about to carry out a tit-for-tat sectarian killing of the Catholic as the odd man out, the one who would have been presumed to be in sympathy with the IRA and all its actions. It was a terrible moment for him, caught between dread and witness, but he did make a motion to step forward. Then, the story goes, in that split second of decision, and in the relative cover of the winter evening darkness, he felt the hand of the Protestant worker next to him take his hand and squeeze it in a signal that said no, don't move, we'll not betray you, nobody need know what faith or party you belong to. All in vain, however, for the man stepped out of the line; but instead of finding a gun at his temple, he was thrown backward and away as the gunmen opened fire on those remaining in the line, for these were not Protestant terrorists, but members, presumably, of the Provisional IRA.

∽

It is difficult at times to repress the thought that history is about as instructive as an abattoir; that Tacitus was right and that peace is merely the desolation left behind after the decisive operations of merciless power. I remember, for example, shocking myself with a thought I had about that friend who was imprisoned in the seventies upon suspicion of having been involved with a political murder: I shocked myself by thinking that even if he were guilty, he might still perhaps be helping the future to be born, breaking the repressive forms and liberating new potential in the only way that worked, that is to say the violent way — which therefore becomes, by extension, the right way. It was like a moment of exposure to interstellar cold, a reminder of the scary element, both inner and outer, in which human beings must envisage and conduct their lives. But it was only a moment. The birth of the future we desire is surely in the contraction which that terrifed Catholic felt on the roadside when another hand gripped his hand, not in the gunfire that followed, so absolute and so desolate, if also so much a part of the music of what happens.

As writers and readers, as sinners and citizens, our realism and our aesthetic sense make us wary of crediting the positive note. The very gunfire braces us and the atrocious confers a worth upon the effort which it calls forth to confront it. We are rightly in awe of the torsions in the poetry of Paul Celan and rightly enamoured of the suspiring voice in Samuel Beckett because these are evidence that art can rise to the occasion and somehow be the corollary of Celan's stricken destiny as Holocaust survivor and Beckett's demure heroism as a member of the French Resistance. Likewise, we are rightly suspicious of that which gives too much consolation in these circumstances; the very extremity of our late twentieth century knowledge puts much of our cultural heritage to an extreme test. Only the very stupid or the very deprived can any longer help knowing that the documents of civilization have been written in blood and tears, blood and tears no less real for being very remote. And when this intellectual predisposition coexists with the actualities of Ulster and Israel and Bosnia and Rwanda and a host of other wounded spots on the face of the earth, the inclination is not only not to credit human nature with much constructive potential but not to credit anything too positive in the work of art.

Which is why for years I was bowed to the desk like some monk bowed over his prie-dieu, some dutiful contemplative pivoting his understanding in an attempt to bear his portion of the weight of the world, knowing himself incapable of heroic virtue or redemptive effect, but constrained by his obedience to his rule to repeat the effort and the posture. Blowing up sparks for a meagre heat. Forgetting faith, straining towards good works. Attending insufficiently to the diamond absolutes, among which must be counted the sufficiency of that which is absolutely imagined. Then finally and happily, and not in obedience to the dolorous circumstances of my native place but in despite of them, I straightened up. I began a few years ago to try to make space in my reckoning and imagining for the marvellous as well as for the murderous. And once again I shall try to represent the import of that changed orientation with a story out of Ireland.

This is a story about another monk holding himself up valiantly in the posture of endurance. It is said that once upon a time St Kevin was kneeling with his arms stretched out in the form of a cross in Glendalough, a monastic site not too far from where we lived in County Wicklow, a place which to this day is one of the most wooded and watery retreats in the whole of the country. Anyhow, as Kevin knelt and prayed, a blackbird mistook his outstretched hand for some kind of roost and swooped down upon it, laid a clutch of eggs in it and proceded to nest in it as if it were the branch of a tree. Then, overcome with pity and constrained by his faith to love the life in all creatures great and small, Kevin stayed immobile for hours and days and nights and weeks, holding out his hand until the eggs hatched and the fledglings grew wings, true to life if subversive of common sense, at the intersection of natural process and the glimpsed ideal, at one and the same time a signpost and a reminder.

Manifesting that order of poetry where we can at last grow up to that which we stored up as we grew.

~~

St Kevin's story is, as I say, a story out of Ireland. But it strikes me that it could equally well come out of India or Africa or the Arctic or the Americas. By which I do not mean merely to consign it to a typology of folktales, or to dispute its value by questioning its culture-bound status within a multi-cultural context. On the contrary, its trustworthiness and its travel-worthiness have to do with its local setting. I can, of course, imagine it being deconstructed nowadays as a paradigm of colonialism, with Kevin figuring as the benign imperialist (or the missionary in the wake of the imperialist), the one who intervenes and appropriates the indigenous life and interferes with its pristine ecology. And I have to admit that there is indeed an irony in the fact that it was such a one who recorded and preserved this instance of the true beauty of the Irish heritage: Kevin's story, after all, appears in the writings of a Norman chronicler, Giraldus Cambrensis, one of the people who invaded Ireland in the twelfth century, one whom the Irish-language annalist Geoffrey Keating would call, five hundred years later, 'the bull of the herd of those who wrote the false history of Ireland'. But even so, I still cannot persuade myself that this manifestation of early Christian civilization should be construed all that simply as a way into whatever is exploitative or barbaric in our history, past and present. The whole conception strikes me rather as being another example of the kind of work I saw a few weeks ago in the small museum in Sparta, on the morning before the news of this year's Nobel prize in literature was announced.

This was art which sprang from a cult very different from the faith espoused by St Kevin. Yet in it there was a representation of a roosted bird and an entranced beast and a self-enrapturing man, except that this time the man was Orpheus and the rapture came from music rather than prayer. The work itself was a small carved relief and I could not help making a sketch of it; but neither could I help copying out the information typed on the card which accompanied and identified the exhibit. The image moved me because of its antiquity and durability, but the description on the card moved me also because it gave a name and credence to that which I see myself as having been engaged upon for the past three decades: 'Votive panel', the identification card said, 'possibly set up to Orpheus by local poet. Local work of the Hellenistic period.'

Once again, I hope I am not being sentimental or simply fetishizing — as we have learnt to say — the local. I wish instead to suggest that images and stories of the kind I am invoking here do function as bearers of value. The century has witnessed the defeat of Nazism by force of arms; but the erosion of the Soviet régimes was caused by, among other things, the sheer persistence, beneath the imposed ideological conformity, of cultural values and psychic resistances of the kind that these stories and images enshrine. Even if we have learned to be rightly and deeply fearful of elevating the cultural forms and conservatisms of any nation into normative and exclusivist systems, even if we have terrible proof that pride in the ethnic and religious heritage can quickly degrade into the fascistic, our vigilance on that score should not displace our love and trust in the good of the indigenous *per se*.

On the contrary, a trust in the staying power and travel-worthiness of such good should encourage us to credit the possibility of a world where respect for the validity of every tradition will issue in the creation and maintenance of a salubrious political space. In spite of devastating and repeated acts of massacre, assassination and extirpation, the huge acts of faith which have marked the new relations between Palestinians and Israelis, Africans and Afrikaners, and the way in which walls have come down in Europe and iron curtains have opened, all this inspires a hope that new possibility can still open up in Ireland as well. The crux of that problem involves an ongoing partition of the island between British and Irish jurisdictions, and an equally persistent partition of the affections in Northern Ireland between the British and Irish heritages; but surely every dweller in the country must hope that the governments involved in its governance can devise institutions which will allow that partition to become a bit more like the net on a tennis court, a demarcation allowing for agile give-and-take, for encounter and contending, prefiguring a future where the vitality that flowed in the beginning from those bracing words 'enemy' and 'allies' might finally derive from a less binary and altogether less binding vocabulary.

∾

When the poet W. B. Yeats stood on this platform more than seventy years ago, Ireland was emerging from the throes of a traumatic civil war that had followed fast on the heels of a war of independence fought against the British. The struggle that ensued had been brief enough; it was over by May, 1923, some seven months before Yeats sailed to Stockholm, but it was bloody, savage and intimate, and for generations to come it would dictate the terms of politics within the twenty-six independent counties of Ireland, that part of the island known first of all as the Irish Free State and then subsequently as the Republic of Ireland.

Yeats barely alluded to the civil war or the war of independence in his Nobel speech. Nobody understood better than he the connection between the construction or destruction of political order and the founding or foundering of cultural life, but on this occasion he chose to talk instead about the Irish Dramatic Movement. His story was about the creative purpose of that movement and its historic good fortune in having not only his own genius to sponsor it, but also the genius of his friends John Millington Synge and Lady Augusta Gregory. He came to Sweden to tell the world that the local work of poets and dramatists had been as important to the transformation of his native place and times as the ambushes of guerrilla armies; and his boast in that elevated prose was essentially the same as the one he would make in verse more than a decade later in his poem 'The Municipal Gallery Revisited'. There Yeats presents himself amongst the portraits and heroic narrative paintings which celebrate the events and personalities of recent history and all of a sudden realizes that something truly epoch-making has occurred: "'This is not,' I say, / 'The dead Ireland of my youth, but an Ireland / The poets have imagined, terrible and gay.'" And the poem concludes with two of the most quoted lines of his entire oeuvre:

> Think where man's glory most begins and ends,
> And say my glory was I had such friends.

And yet, expansive and thrilling as these lines are, they are an instance of poetry flourishing itself rather than proving itself, they are the poet's lap of honour, and in this respect if in no other they resemble what I am doing in this lecture.

In fact, I should also quote here on my own behalf some other words from the poem: 'You that would judge me, do not judge alone / This book or that.' Instead, I ask you to do what Yeats asked his readers to do and think of the achievement of Irish poets and dramatists and novelists over the past forty years, among whom I am proud to count great friends. In literary matters, Ezra Pound advised against accepting the opinion of those 'who haven't themselves produced significant work,' and it is advice I have been privileged to follow, since it is the good opinion of notable workers — and not just those in my own country — that has fortified my endeavour since I began to write in Belfast more than thirty years ago.

Yeats, however, was by no means all flourish. To the credit of poetry in our century there must surely be entered in any reckoning his two great sequences of poems entitled 'Nineteen Hundred and Nineteen' and 'Meditations in Time of Civil War', the latter of which contains the famous lyric about the bird's nest at his window, where a starling or stare had built in a crevice of the old wall. The poet was living then in a Norman tower which had been very much a part of the military history of the country in earlier times, and as his thoughts turned upon the irony of civilizations being consolidated by violent and powerful conquerors who end up commissioning the artists and the architects, he began to associate the sight of a mother bird feeding its young with the image of the honey-bee, an image deeply lodged in poetic tradition and always suggestive of the ideal of an industrious, harmonious, nurturing commonwealth:

> The bees build in the crevices
> Of loosening masonry, and there
> The mother birds bring grubs and flies.

My wall is loosening; honey-bees,
Come build in the empty house of the stare.

We are closed in, and the key is turned
On our uncertainty; somewhere
A man is killed, or a house burned,
Yet no clear fact to be discerned:
Come build in the empty house of the stare.

A barricade of stone or of wood;
Some fourteen days of civil war;
Last night they trundled down the road
That dead young soldier in his blood:
Come build in the empty house of the stare.

We had fed the heart on fantasies,
The heart's grown brutal from the fare;
More substance in our enmities
Than in our love; O honey-bees,
Come build in the empty house of the stare.

I have heard this poem repeated often, in whole and in part, by people in Ireland over the past twenty-five years, and no wonder, for it is as tender-minded towards life itself as St Kevin was and as tough-minded about what happens in and to life as Homer. It knows that the massacre will happen again on the roadside, that the workers in the minibus are going to be lined up and shot down just after quitting time; but it also credits as a reality the squeeze of the hand, the actuality of sympathy and protectiveness between living creatures. It satisfies the contradictory needs which consciousness experiences at times of extreme crisis, the need on the one hand for a truth-telling that will be hard and retributive, and on the other hand, the need not to harden the mind to a point where it denies its own yearnings for sweetness and trust. It is a proof that poetry can be equal to *and* true at the same time, an example of that completely adequate poetry which the Russian woman sought from Anna Akhmatova and which William Wordsworth produced at a corresponding moment of historical crisis and personal dismay almost exactly two hundred years ago.

∾

When the bard Demodokos sings of the fall of Troy and of the slaughter that accompanied it, Odysseus weeps and Homer says that his tears were like the tears of a wife on a battlefield weeping for the death of a fallen husband. His epic simile continues, in Robert Fitzgerald's translation:

> At the sight of the man panting and dying there,
> she slips down to enfold him, crying out;
> then feels the spears, prodding her back and shoulders,
> and goes bound into slavery and grief.
> Piteous weeping wears away her cheeks:
> but no more piteous than Odysseus' tears,
> cloaked as they were, now, from the company.

Even today, three thousand years later, as we channel-surf over so much live coverage of contemporary savagery, highly informed but nevertheless in danger of growing immune, familiar to the point of overfamiliarity with old newsreels of the concentration camp and the gulag, Homer's image can still bring us to our senses. The callousness of those spear shafts on the woman's back and shoulders survives time and translation. The image has that documentary adequacy which answers all that we know about the intolerable.

But there is another kind of adequacy which is specific to lyric poetry. This has to do with the 'temple inside our hearing' which the passage of the poem calls into being. It is an adequacy deriving from what Mandelstam called 'the steadfastness of speech articulation,' from the resolution and independence which the entirely realized poem sponsors. It has as much to do with the energy released by linguistic fission and fusion, with the buoyancy generated by cadence and tone and rhyme and stanza, as it has to do with the poem's concerns or the poet's truthfulness. In fact, in lyric poetry, truthfulness becomes recognizable as a ring of truth within the medium itself. And it is the unappeasable pursuit of this note, a note tuned to its most extreme in Emily Dickinson and Paul Celan and orchestrated to its most opulent in John Keats, it is this which keeps the poet's ear straining to hear the totally persuasive voice behind all the other informing voices.

Which is a way of saying that I have never quite climbed down from the arm of that sofa. I may have grown more attentive to the news and more alive to the world history and world-sorrow behind it. But the thing uttered by the speaker I strain towards is still not quite the story of what is going on; it is more reflexive than that, because as a poet I am in fact straining towards a strain, in the sense that the effort is to repose in the stability conferred by a musically satisfying order of sounds. As if the ripple at its widest desired to be verified by a reformation of itself, to be drawn in and drawn out through its point of origin.

I also strain towards this in the poetry I read. And I find it, for example, in the repetition of that refrain of Yeats's, 'Come build in the empty house of the stare,' with its tone of supplication, its pivots of strength in the words 'build' and 'house' and its acknowledgement of dissolution in the word 'empty'. I find it also in the triangle of forces held in equilibrium by the triple rhyme of 'fantasies' and 'enmities' and 'honey-bees', and in the sheer in-placeness of the whole poem as a given form within the language. Poetic form is both the ship and the anchor. It is at once a buoyancy and a holding, allowing for the simultaneous gratification of whatever is centrifugal and centripetal in mind and body. And it is by such means that Yeats's work does what the necessary poetry always does, which is to touch the base of our sympathetic nature while taking in at the same time the unsympathetic reality of the world to which that nature is constantly exposed. The form of the poem, in other words, is crucial to poetry's power to do the thing which always is and always will be to poetry's credit: the power to persuade that vulnerable part of our consciousness of its rightness in spite of the evidence of wrongness all around it, the power to remind us that we are hunters and gatherers of values, that our very solitudes and distresses are creditable, in so far as they, too, are an earnest of our veritable human being.